HERITAGE

The VIKINGS *in Britain*

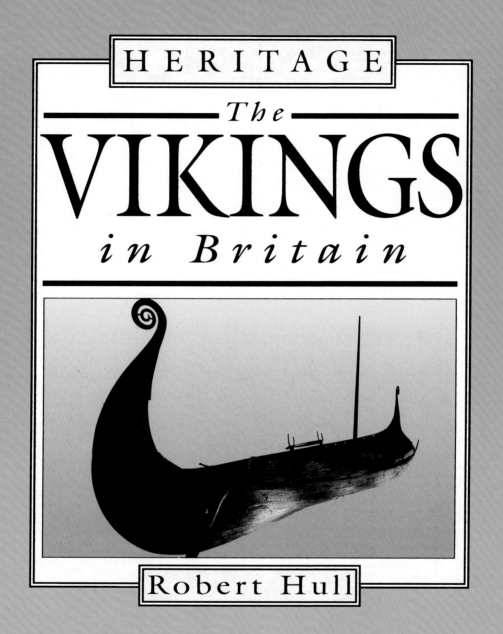

Robert Hull

WAYLAND

Heritage

The Anglo-Saxons
The Celts in Britain
The Romans in Britain
The Tudors
The Victorians
The Vikings in Britain

Cover pictures: A Viking farm at Jarlshof in Shetland (main picture). Jewellery from Scotland (left); a leather boot found at Jorvik and a runestone (right).

Editors: Joanna Bentley and Rosemary Ashley
Designer: Jean Wheeler

First published in 1997 by
Wayland (Publishers) Limited,
61 Western Road, Hove,
East Sussex, BN3 1JD, England

British Library Cataloguing in Publication Data

Hull, Robert
  The Vikings in Britain. - (Heritage)
  1. Vikings - Great Britain - Juvenile literature
  2. Vikings - Great Britain -Social life and customs - Juvenile literature
  3. Great Britain - History - To 1066 - Juvenile literature
  I.Title
  941'.01'089395

  ISBN 0750216565

Typeset by Jean Wheeler

Printed and bound in Italy by G. Canale & C.S.p.A., Turin

Contents

chapter one

WHO WERE
THE VIKINGS?

The Vikings were Scandinavian farmers and fishermen who became explorers, traders, raiders and settlers. One meaning of 'vik' is a creek or sea inlet; 'vikings' could mean the men who kept their boats in creeks, ready to set sail: ready to go exploring and raiding.

◄ *This memorial stone carved with runes (the Viking alphabet) shows how far the Vikings travelled. It was erected by a Viking wife, Estrid, in memory of her husband, Osten. He had visited Jerusalem and died in Greece.*

They set sail from Scandinavia, from the countries we now call Sweden, Denmark and Norway. They were three groups but really only one people, who spoke the same language, Old Norse. Until about the eighth century, this Scandinavian people farmed and traded peacefully.

From about the eighth century, a passion for voyaging seemed to take hold of the Vikings. With wonderfully advanced ships, they made long voyages to trade with other peoples. They also made voyages to grab loot: smash-and-grab raids. Later, they made voyages to settle in new lands. And in the tenth century, kings took fleets and large armies to conquer whole countries and build an empire.

A Russian monk, Nestor, wrote that in 880 a Swedish Viking, Oleg, 'set himself up as prince of Kiev, and declared that it should be the mother of Russian cities'.

▼ A map showing the routes travelled by the Vikings to Britain and Ireland, and to the rest of Europe.

▼ This is the most westerly part of Norway, from where Viking ships voyaged to the north of Britain.

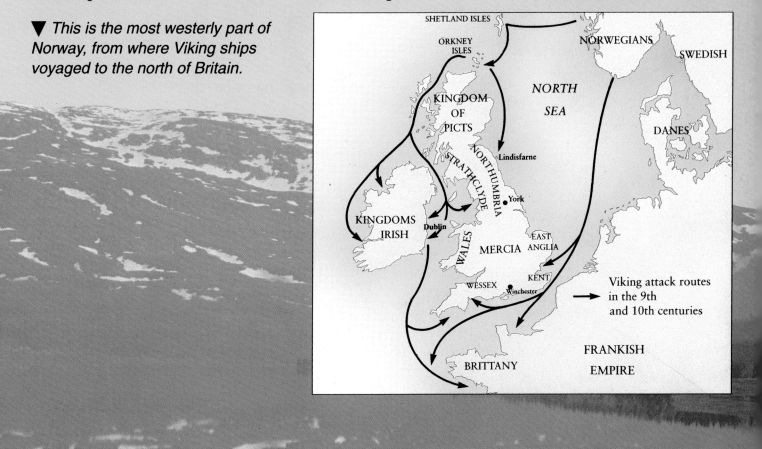

Viking attack routes in the 9th and 10th centuries

An Irish writer described the Vikings' return from raids on Spain: 'The Norsemen brought a great host of Moors in captivity with them to Ireland ... Long were these blue men in Ireland.'

▼ *A hoard of Viking silver was found on this beach in Orkney. The hoard contained brooches, arm-rings and even Arabic coins, brought by Viking traders.*

Vikings in Britain

The Danish and Norse Vikings came to Britain in the eighth century. Norsemen (Norwegian Vikings) settled in the Orkney and Shetland Islands. From there they attacked the western islands of Scotland and other parts of Britain.

Norsemen and Danes grabbed land on the east coast of Ireland, and built houses, workshops, and warehouses. The area became a trading centre, then a town, eventually called Dublin.

The raiders brought to Britain fire and murder and cruelty. But they also traded, and farmed the land. Much of north-west England was settled by Norse farmers from Ireland.

York and Dublin became important Viking cities and manufacturing centres. Viking leaders became kings and rulers in many parts of the country.

Britain is full of signs of our Viking past: towns and villages with Viking names, remains of Viking farms and houses – mainly in the north and the Orkney Islands. In churchyards there are stones and crosses that Viking craftsmen carved. In museums there are swords that they hurled into rivers, coins they buried in a hurry, brooches, combs, rings.

▶ *These scales were used to weigh silver. The Vikings valued silver by weight, both silver coins and 'hack-silver', which was silver that had been chopped up to be re-used.*

chapter two

WHEN DID THE VIKINGS
RAID BRITAIN?

▲ *This hoard of Viking silver was buried on the banks of a river in Lancashire, in about AD 900. Much of the silver is 'hack-silver', cut up to be re-used.*

▼ *The abbey on the island of Iona, off the Scottish coast, was an easy target for the Vikings*

The first Viking raid was an attack on Lindisfarne monastery, in Northumbria in AD 793. They burnt and murdered, grabbing the monastery's silver and taking monks for slaves. The following year, they attacked nearby Jarrow monastery, but a storm smashed their ships, and the survivors were put to death.

Raiding all over Britain

The years after 794 were a time of terrible Viking attacks on many parts of Britain and Ireland. They raided the Orkney Islands, Shetland Islands, the Hebrides, Iona, the Isle of Man, Wales and Ireland. The Vikings did not come every year, or even very often, but they were now a menace to all western Europe. Charlemagne, King of the Franks, organized a fleet in the English Channel against them. King Offa of Kent did the same.

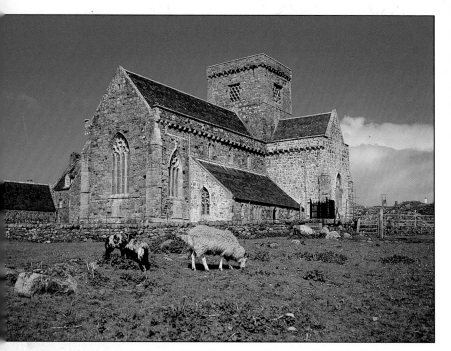

A history of Ulster, called The Annals, has this entry for the year 820: 'The sea poured torrents of foreigners over Erin (Ireland) so that no harbour or stronghold was without waves of Northmen and pirates.'

◀ *This is the beach on Holy Island, in Northumbria, where the Vikings first landed to raid the monastery of Lindisfarne.*

The Vikings burnt churches and killed priests. They were not Christian, and church treasures of gold and silver were easy loot.

From AD 850 the Vikings built winter camps – a worrying sign. From winter camps they went raiding and pillaging more easily, without sailing back home.

But in some of the bigger battles between 840 and 860 the Vikings were badly beaten. For a while they were more successful in Europe. The same bands of warriors raided in different countries. Hoards of coins left in Ireland show that the Viking who buried them had been to England and southwest France (Aquitaine).

More than 300 years after the attack on Lindisfarne, a monk, Symeon of Durham, wrote a history of Northumbria. He was still horrified at the memory of the Vikings' arrival: 'In this year, the Pagans from the northern part of the world came like stinging hornets to Britain... like ravening wolves, plundering, devouring, slaughtering... seizing the treasure of the holy church. Some of the monks they kill outright, others they carry away with them.'

Dividing up England: the Danelaw

After AD 860 writers all over Europe talked of bigger Viking fleets, of between 150 and 200 ships. In 865 and 872, the Anglo-Saxon Chronicle records that 'great armies' of Vikings invaded England. The Vikings stayed the winter in East Anglia. Their aim now was conquest. They wanted to take the land, to live on it and farm it.

By 874 their 'great army' had conquered the English kingdoms of Mercia, Northumbria and East Anglia, including London. English kings were put to death.

▲ This painting on the wall of a Yorkshire church shows Edmund, king of East Anglia, being shot by Viking archers.

The Vikings were often cruel. A saga (story) describes how two English rivals for the kingdom of Northumbria, were killed by the fearsome 'bloodeagle' method: their lungs were torn out and pinned across their backs like wings. Some writers say that this only happened in Viking sagas; and that these bloodthirsty stories were not true. Others say 'blood-eagleing' really happened.

But Wessex, led by King Aethelbert and later the young Alfred, fought back. In 886 King Alfred attacked the Vikings and captured London. Alfred made an agreement with the Viking leader, Guthorm. They drew a boundary between English and Danish land. The Danish part came to be called the Danelaw.

The Danelaw becomes English again

Fighting continued between Viking armies and the English. The kings of Wessex aimed to get the Danelaw back. Alfred died in 899, but between about 900 and 937, the Wessex English reconquered the Danelaw.

Then in 939 Norse Vikings from Dublin invaded, and beat the English. England became one country and the Norse Vikings stayed on. They became English.

Raiding to build an empire

In about 980, the Viking attacks began again. This time, the Viking bands were more like real armies. They also had bases in Normandy, close to the English coast.

For the first time the English paid money to the Vikings, to stay away. This protection money was called 'danegeld'. More and more was paid over the next few years; by 1040 huge amounts of silver had been handed over.

The Vikings did not stay away. A new Viking leader, Sweyn, with his son Cnut, attacked in 1013. Sweyn died in 1014, but fighting went on until the death of the English king, Edmund. After Edmund's death, the English accepted the Viking Cnut as King of England. England had become part of the Danish Empire.

▲ *A drawing of King Cnut and his English wife at Winchester. Cnut had become a devout Christian and he depended on leaders of the Christian Church to help him rule firmly.*

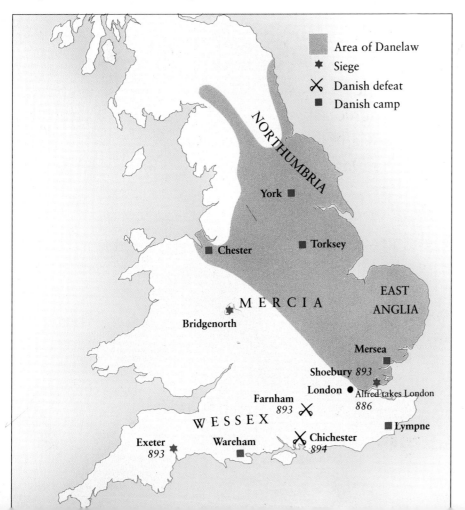

Area of Danelaw
★ Siege
✗ Danish defeat
■ Danish camp

NORTHUMBRIA

York ■

■ Chester   ■ Torksey

M E R C I A   EAST ANGLIA

Bridgenorth

Mersea ■

Shoebury *893*

London ● Alfred takes London
Farnham *886*
893 ✗

W E S S E X

Exeter   Wareham   ✗ Chichester
893   *894*

■ Lympne

◀ *A map showing the area of Viking rule (the Danelaw) in 886. King Alfred re-conquered much of the Danelaw and after his death it was all regained by the English.*

For 894 the Anglo-Saxon Chronicle says: 'And when the Viking army which had besieged Exeter turned back for home, they ravaged up (pillaged) in Sussex near Chichester and the townsmen put them to flight and killed many hundreds of them and captured some of their ships.'

chapter three

WHERE DID THE VIKINGS SETTLE IN BRITAIN?

▼ *Shetland, where Norse Vikings landed and where they settled. They would have felt at home in these wild, northern islands.*

About a day's sail west from Norway, the low outline of Shetland appears on the horizon. These islands, where the Norse Vikings beached their boats, about the end of the eighth century, would have reminded them of home.

The Picts lived on Shetland. They had small settlements, and a Christian church. No one knows exactly what happened when the Vikings met the Picts, but the Picts' church was destroyed, and the Vikings settled there. They settled on other parts of Shetland too, and on the Orkney Islands.

Archaeologists have found Viking farms at Jarlshof on Shetland, and at Birsay and Buckquoy on Orkney. And others have been found from clues in the 'Orkneyinga Saga', a history of Orkney which names actual farms and locations.

▼ *The ruins of Earl Thorfinn's palace on the island of Brough of Birsay, in Orkney. Thorfinn was the Viking ruler of the Western Isles from 1014 to 1064.*

Clues from place names

In England, even in 'the Danelaw', there are not many buildings that archaeologists can point to and say 'that is a Viking farm'. But place names are a good clue to which parts of England the Vikings settled.

Wherever you see a 'by' at the end of a name for a place, the Vikings were probably there. The word is Scandinavian and means a group of houses or a village.

In the north and east of England, there are places ending in 'thorp', meaning a small settlement. There are many 'thwaites' and 'tofts' as well; in Danish 'thwaite' was a clearing for pasture, and 'toft' a piece of ground. The Lake District is full of 'thwaite' places.

chapter four

HOW DID THE
VIKINGS LIVE?

▶ *The ruins of a Viking farm built in the ninth-century at Jarlshof on Shetland. It's Norse name was Svinburgh, meaning 'fort of pigs'. The farm was lived in until the fifteenth century.*

The Norse settlers on Orkney and Shetland were farmers, but they were Vikings too, and still went raiding. The Orkneyinga Saga describes how one Viking farmer on Orkney lived: 'He spent winter at home on Gairsay, feasting about eighty men at his own expense... After the spring sowing, he would go off plundering in the Hebrides and in Ireland, on what he called his 'spring trip', then back home just after midsummer, where he stayed till the cornfields had been reaped... After that he would go on his 'autumn trip'.

The Orkney and Shetland Islands suited the Vikings. The landscape, the weather, the harsh life of these northern islands were like those at home in Norway. They were settlers here, not raiders.

The Viking farmer's life

Viking farms were often built on the ruins of earlier buildings, perhaps re-using the stone. They built farmhouses with low stone walls. A farm would have a 'hall house' for living in, often oblong-shaped. Then there would be separate outbuildings: a byre (for cattle), a stable, a barn for threshing and storing corn, and perhaps a bathhouse.

Viking town life

But many Vikings lived further south, inland amongst the English, and in towns. Their lives were different from those of the Orkney farmers.

When the Vikings captured Eoforwic (York) in 866, it must have seemed a disaster to the English residents. But over the next thirty years the Vikings who came and settled there built a defensive wall, new streets, and another bridge. They called the 'Vikingized' town Jorvik.

We know many things about Jorvik, because the wet ground has preserved parts of the town. Near the Rivers Ouse and Foss in Jorvik many things that would normally decay have been preserved by the damp conditions.

▼ *Archaeologists excavating a wattle-lined pit in Coppergate, York (Jorvik), after a factory was demolished in 1976. The Vikings probably used the pit for storage.*

Viking Jorvik was a very busy place, crammed with people. New thatched timber houses were built for the newcomers. To get more people in, the houses were set sideways to the streets.

Behind the houses, stretching down towards the river, were workshops, then rubbish pits and wells, and warehouses. Archaeologists have worked out that by 1066 (when the Normans came) York had about 10,000 people living in nearly 2,000 houses.

In Jorvik, there were tanneries, for preparing leather, and workshops for making boots, shoes, belts and sheaths for knives. Blacksmiths made horseshoes, padlocks and keys, swords, axes and nails. Jewellers sold brooches, and ornaments made of copper, lead, silver and gold.

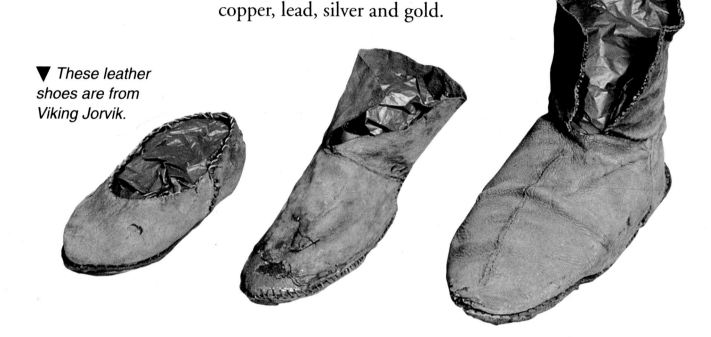

▼ *These leather shoes are from Viking Jorvik.*

► *Brooches made from silver and lead, were crafted in the workshops at Jorvik.*

Women spun flax and wool and wove cloth in their own houses.

Workers' houses were dark, cramped and smelly. The floor was of earth, with a smoky fire in the middle. There might have been a table and stools, and a bench along the wall for sleeping on.

In Dublin similar clues about Viking town life have been found, and many more weapons. Perhaps this is because there was more fighting: in the late tenth and early eleventh centuries the Vikings were attacked by the Irish and many were driven away.

The sagas often refer to women's appearance, and their clothes and jewellery: 'Their jewels, their saddles beautifully woven and foreign, their beautifully woven cloths of all kinds, their satins and silks so pleasing and variegated, scarlet and green...'

The Viking houses in Dublin were rectangular and single-storey. The 'walls' were lines of posts with thin strips of ash or hazel woven between them like baskets. This method was called 'wattle and post' construction. There might be a hearth bordered with stones in the middle of the floor. The floor would be carpeted with rushes.

All this information from the Orkney Islands, Jorvik, and Dublin tells us that the British Vikings were no longer just hunter-farmers who went raiding and pillaging in their ships. They were merchants, craftsmen, smiths, shipowners and sailors, coinmakers, and warriors, fishermen, farmers, and so on. Their lives were more complicated than the early Vikings', but less harsh.

◀ *Swords made by Viking smiths.*

chapter five

WHAT ARTS AND SKILLS DID THE VIKINGS HAVE?

▼ *This perfectly preserved ship, known as the Oseberg Boat, was found in Norway. The ship contained the skeletons of three people. With them were objects for use in the next world (after death), including buckets, spades, beds and a cart.*

The Vikings had many skills; they were fine smiths and poets, but their greatest skill was shipbuilding. They built amazing boats. The Vikings were successful as traders and raiders mainly because their ships were ahead of their time.

The early Vikings had oar-powered boats, with as many as thirty oars on each side. They had different kinds of boats for fishing, local trade, long expeditions, and war.

Sometime before 800 the Vikings added a mast and sail to some of their boats, and they invented the keel – a piece of wood attached along the length of the boat, underneath it. The keel made the boats easier to handle in strong currents, and using the sail to power the boats they could make way in heavy seas and against headwinds.

Viking longships were a frightening sight. One saga writer says: 'From a long way off, the boats seemed to be made of flames, not wood.' And: 'When they came close to the islands, they saw a dragon head which shone like gold. They saw that there were twelve ships with the dragon, all covered with black tents. Light came from under the tents where the men sat drinking.'

◄ *The figurehead of a Viking ship was often carved in the shape of a fierce creature – to calm the waves or frighten off sea-monsters. The 'prow-carpenters' who did this work were better paid than other carpenters.*

▼ *The beautifully carved prow of the Oseberg boat.*

Viking ships were made mostly of oak. They were painted, the prow sometimes in gold. The sail too, was coloured, blue or red, sometimes in stripes.

Below the waterline a different method was used. Strips of wood were tied to the framework of the boat with roots of spruce. This was one of the Vikings' most brilliant inventions. It meant that when the ship was being battered by strong seas, the part of the boat below the waterline could flex and give.

Out into the Atlantic

With their advanced ships, the Vikings could now take on the Atlantic. They could sail west to the Shetland Islands, and round Scotland to Ireland.

19

Viking ships in Britain

Thousands of Viking ships came to Britain during the Viking Age; and many must have been wrecked or abandoned here. But only a few small dugout boats have been found from Viking times, and a few fragments of bigger ones.

▼ *This picture stone from Sweden is carved to show Viking men in a boat.*

The Viking boats that first attacked Britain in the eighth century were mainly warships, called 'longships'. They had especially big warships, too, called 'dragon ships'. Later, they used other ships as well, to carry settlers and their gear. One was the 'knorr', a kind of cargo ship. The knorr could carry thirty people, as well as animals, barrels of water and beer, and provisions like smoked fish, salted meat, and fruit.

Viking ships of all kinds could travel in only a few feet of water, so Viking attackers could sail far inland up shallow English rivers. They could carry cargoes of wine and spices right into Jorvik, to the town's quay. But the boats didn't need harbours. They could be drawn up out of the water on riverbanks or beaches anywhere, to land warriors, animals and equipment.

The Vikings loved their boats. Two of them were named: 'Deer of the Sea', and 'Raven of the Wind'. They wrote poems about them. In poems their ships are 'surf-dragons', or 'ocean-striding bison'.

Viking artistry
The Vikings' boats were worked on by brilliant woodcarvers. The Viking smiths' work in bronze, silver and gold was like the woodcarver's, full of winding intricate designs.

▲ *A stone capital – from the top of a stone column – from Norwich Cathedral in south-east England. The capital also shows the same kind of twisting shapes as the carving.*

▲ *This intricate carving has interlacing, twisting shapes, which the Vikings were particularly fond of using for decoration.*

Viking silver and gold rings and brooches were just as full of fascinating designs, often using patterns of weaving animals. Viking craftsmen loved making and decorating weapons. Some of them were thrown into rivers, as gifts to a god.

▶ *This beautiful gold brooch, with its intricate twisting decoration, was made by a Viking craftsman.*

chapter six

WHAT RELIGIOUS BELIEFS DID THE VIKINGS HAVE?

The Vikings believed in three great worlds. In the middle was Earth, called Midgard. Under Earth, to the north, was Nifelheim, a place of mist, frozen rivers and endless dark, home of the dead and the monster called Hel. Above Earth was Asgard, shining home of the gods.

Midgard was made from the body of a dead giant, Ymir. Rocks were made from his teeth, clouds from his brains, mountains from his bones. Midgard was protected by a fence made from Ymir's eyebrows.

In Asgard lived two races of gods, the Vanir and the Aesir. In one part of Asgard was Valhalla, the 'hall of those who die in battle' – the Viking heaven. Those who died of old age or illness went to Nifelheim; death in battle was the only way to get to Valhalla.

▲ A rune stone from Sweden. It shows the eight-legged horse, Sleipnir, which belonged to the chief Viking god, Odin. Sleipnir could travel at incredible speed, and journey to the land of the dead.

Viking gods

The main Viking gods were Odin, Thor, and Frigg. Odin was chief of the group of gods called the Aesir. He was the terrifying god of battles, wisdom and poetry. He had only one eye; he sacrificed the other in exchange for wisdom.

The bronze heads of two Viking gods, Thor and Frey. They are both depicted with moustaches and beards.

Frigg was Odin's wife, the mother of the gods. Thor was the son of Odin and Frigg. He was the popular red-bearded god of thunder, and rode in a chariot pulled by two goats; as the chariot drove along, lightning would flash from its wheels. Thor could kill one of his goats to eat, then bring it back to life by touching its skin with his hammer, called Mjollnir.

There were other important gods. Loki was a deceitful god. Frey was god of fertility, and his twin sister Freya was goddess of beauty and war. Frey had the best of all Viking ships, Skibaldnir, which could carry all the gods, and still be folded away into a purse.

In most of Britain these old gods have left only their names behind them – in our days of the week. Wednesday is 'Odin's (or Woden's) day'; Thursday is 'Thor's day'; and Friday is 'Frey's (or Frigg's) day'.

According to one writer the Vikings sometimes made living sacrifices. 'Nine heads are offered of every kind of male creature', including human. A Christian told the writer that he had seen seventy corpses of dogs, horses and men, hanging from trees in a grove.

Viking burials in Britain

Many Viking graves have been found on the Isle of Man. At Balladoole, a low ridge of earth is marked by stones. Though no wood has been found, 300 nails have, lying in the outline of a boat. Rich Vikings, as well as chiefs and queens, were often buried in boats, to carry them to Valhalla, in the next world.

The boat grave at Balladoole shows how a dead Viking was sent cruising to Valhalla. With him went personal items: a knife, a cloak pin, and a flint 'lighter'. He also took a cauldron containing drink, and horse gear. There was a young woman nearby. Perhaps she was sacrificed, though there was no sign of a violent death.

▶ *The boat-shaped Viking burial ground at Balladoole, on the Isle of Man.*

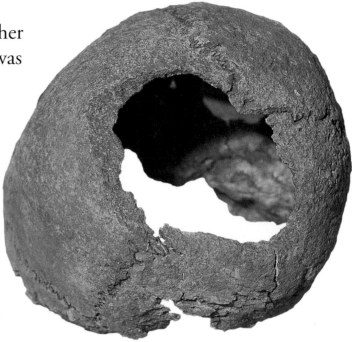

But there were signs of violent death at another burial place, Ballateare. Here, a rich farmer was buried with a sword, some 'killed' spears (broken so as to be harmless), an ox, a horse, a sheep, and a dog, and a young woman with the top of her skull sliced off.

These burials show that some Vikings in the second half of the ninth century were still pagan. They believed in Valhalla, and in the old Norse gods. They thought the world would be destroyed when terrible monsters were set free by the gods.

▲ *The skull of a woman from the Viking ship-burial at Ballateare, on the Isle of Man. She was sacrificed in a horrible way – the top of her head was sliced off.*

▲ *This carved stone in an Isle of Man church shows the god Odin being attacked by a wolf. One of Odin's ravens sits on his shoulder.*

Christian Vikings

The Vikings in Britain gradually became Christian. For a time, they must have had a muddle of beliefs, half Christian, half Viking.

By the tenth century, in the north of England and the old Danelaw, there are clear signs of Viking Christian belief. A church door has a Viking ship of iron nailed across it. Tombstones show that Vikings had Christian burials. By the eleventh century the Vikings of the Shetland and Orkney Islands too had become Christian. The old religion had finally faded.

chapter seven

WHAT STORIES
DID THE VIKINGS TELL?

On howling winter nights the Vikings listened to sagas about their favourite gods. They liked mischievous Loki, and, even more, great-hearted Thor with his magic hammer, his iron gloves, and the belt that doubled his strength when he put it on.

The Vikings listened around the hearthfire in small houses, at great feasts in halls, and on icy nights in their open boats. No poet or storyteller read to them. None of the stories, poems or history was written down until after 'The Viking Age'. They were all remembered by heart.

There were hundreds of tales of magic, adventure and horror. There was the wolf that chased the sun and moon, the giant so big that Thor, late at night, crept into his glove to sleep there, thinking it was a barn. There was a story about stars tumbling from the sky at Ragnarok, the end of the world.

▲ *Thor holds Mjollnir, his magic hammer. This bronze image from Iceland shows a hammer which also looks like an upside-down Christian cross.*

The Orkneyinga Saga describes a gruesome accident: 'Sigurd had their heads strapped to the victors' saddles, to show off their victory. On the way back, as Sigurd leaned forward to spur his horse, he struck his calf against a tooth sticking out of his victim's mouth, and it gave him a scratch. The wound became infected, and brought about Sigurd's death.'

Sagas and poems

The Vikings also told tales of their own raids and explorations. These stories, called sagas, were written down in Iceland, between the eleventh and thirteenth centuries. They tell us a great deal about how the Vikings lived.

One part of the Orkneyinga Saga describes a typical raid: 'They attacked Wales, going ashore at a place called Jarlness. One morning they came to a settlement which offered hardly any resistance. The farmers ran for their lives as Svein and his men looted the whole settlement and burned six farms before breakfast.' The poet with them on the raid immediately celebrated the event in words.

The Orkneyinga Saga is about life in the Orkney Islands: 'Einar was the first man to dig peat for fuel, firewood being scarce on the island.'

But the saga is also full of travels, raids, battles at sea, sieges in France, crusades, feasts, burning and torture, hired killings, miraculous escapes, and gruesome happenings.

In Britain Viking poetry must all have been oral: composed aloud and recited from memory. When written down later it became wonderful, magic poetry, bloodcurdling at times, but with lots of common sense as well: 'Before proceeding up the hall, study all the doorways. You never know when an enemy will be present.' And 'Confide in one, not two. Tell three, and the world knows.'

▼ *In Christian Iceland, the Viking sagas were often written down in illuminated (illustrated) manuscripts like this one, which dates from the fourteenth century.*

27

chapter eight

WHAT HAPPENED TO THE
VIKINGS IN BRITAIN?

Many Vikings came to Britain and left to sail to Iceland, and further. But many stayed and added their Viking genes, habits, skills and beliefs to the mixture of peoples called British.

In the Danelaw and northern Britain, Vikings and English worked and lived alongside each other, and married. Each people probably understood the other's language. As time went on their lives and their languages merged into each other.

▲ *The great Viking Cathedral of St Magnus, in Kirkwall, Orkney. The cathedral was founded in 1137.*

A sign of this living together can be seen in place names. There are many places with names that are half Viking, half English, like Grimston, from 'Grim', a Viking personal name, and 'tun', Old English for 'town'.

A Viking country

For about twenty years, from 1017, the Danish king Cnut was also king of England. By this time the Vikings in England had lost some of their Viking habits. Their old sailing skills weren't needed so much. They didn't need to fight as often. They gave up their old beliefs and became Christian. They built churches. When they started to use writing, they wrote English English, not Viking English.

Further north, in the Orkney and Shetland Islands, Viking life went on in the old way. The people built and farmed and fished as they did when they arrived in the late eighth century. They still spoke the Norse language: it was used in the Orkney and Shetland Islands up to the seventeenth century. But they too became Christian. In 1137 a great cathedral was built in Kirkwall, capital of the Orkneys.

Viking words
Everyday English is full of Viking language. For instance, are you awkward, odd, sly, weak? Do you gape and scowl, guess or glitter, or give or take? The Vikings brought these words into our language.

▼ *These round houses at Jarlshof were built by the Picts who lived there before the Vikings came and settled on their land. Jarlshof was the first village in Britain to be identified as Viking.*

As the Vikings settled alongside the English, more Viking words crossed over into the English language. Sometimes the English gave up their own word, for instance 'sweoster' for the Viking word ('sister').

In the Orkneys they have Viking words for different kinds of rain: a driv, a fug, a murr, a hagger, a dag. The Lancashire dialect has lovely Viking words: if you have a 'claggy lug', you have a waxy ear.

If Viking words are all round us, how can we identify them? With one or two groups of words we can tell just by looking. One giveaway group is words beginning with the 'sk' sound. These are all of Viking origin: skim, skitter, skelter, skip, scatter, skirt, sky, skin, scoff, scab, scale, scar, screech.

GLOSSARY

Archaeologists People who study objects and remains from ancient times.

Cauldron A large, heavy pot used for heating liquids.

Chariot A two-wheeled vehicle used in wars in ancient times.

Commemorate To honour the memory of someone.

Danegeld The money, or tax, which the English paid to the Vikings as 'protection money', to stop them from attacking them.

Danelaw The parts of ninth-century England where Viking laws and customs were followed.

Dialect Language spoken in a particular area.

Excavated Dug out.

Fertility The production of healthy crops.

Figurehead A carved figure on the stem (prow) of a boat.

Flax A plant grown for its fibres which make a material called linen.

Genes Parts of our body that account for hereditary characteristics.

Hoard A hidden store of goods.

Loot Stolen goods.

Monastery A building where monks lived and worked. Besides prayer and study, some monks would farm the monastery lands,

Moors People from North Africa who invaded Spain in ancient times.

Norsemen The Vikings who came from Norway.

Old Norse The language spoken by all groups of Vikings.

Oral By word of mouth.

Pagan Referring to a non-Christian religion or person.

Runes The characters (letters) of the Viking alphabet.

Picts The people who lived in Northern Britain from the 1st to 4th centuries AD.

Pillaging Robbing.

Sacrificed Killed as an offering to the gods.

Sagas Ancient Viking stories.

Smiths People skilled in making objects from metal.

Traits Distinguishing features or characteristics.

Wattle Building material made from interwoven twigs and branches

BOOKS TO READ

Over 900 years ago with the Vikings by Hazel Mary Martell (Zoë Books, 1993)
Viking Invaders and Settlers by Tony Triggs (Wayland 1992)
The Vikings by Jason Hook (Wayland, 1993)
The Vikings by Struan Reid (Belitha Press, 1993)
The Vikings and Jorvik by Hazel Mary Martell (Zoë Books, 1993)
Vikings by Robert Nicolson & Claire Watts (Watts Books, 1991)
Vikings by J.D. Clare (Bodley Head, 1991)
What do we know about the Vikings? by Hazel Mary Martell
  (Simon & Schuster, 1992)

PLACES TO VISIT

Jarlshof Museum
Virkie, Shetland Isles
Scotland

The museum displays a special exhibition of Viking material found on Shetland.

Jorvik Viking Centre
Coppergate, York

The Centre is on the site of a Viking settlement, Jorvik, which was excavated in the 1960s. Visitors are taken on a journey through the Viking history of York. Many examples of Viking objects found on the site are displayed at the Centre.

National Museum of Ireland
Kildare Street
Dublin

The museum displays a special exhibition of Viking material.

Tankerness House Museum
Kirkwall
Orkney

Collections tell the story of life in Orkney, including the Viking period.

You can also visit Viking sites on the Shetland and Orkney Islands and the Isle of Man.

INDEX

Numbers in **bold** refer to pictures

Picture acknowledgements
The publishers would like to thank the following for permission to reproduce their pictures: Ancient Art and Architecture Collection 4-5, 6-7, 17(lower), 19(top), 23; British Library 11; C.M. Dixon cover, 4, 9, 10, 21(all), 22, 24, 25(both); Eye Ubiquitous /P. Thomson 12; Michael Holford 8(top), 20; Ann Ronan at Image Select 19(lower), /R. Gaillard 26; Scotland in Focus /J. Weir cover (main picture) and right; Scottish Highland Photo Library 8(lower), /H. Webster 13, /J. Kissack 14, /R. Weir 28, /J. Kissack 29; Werner Forman Archive title page, 7, 18, 27; York Archaeological Trust cover,15,16(both), 17. The maps on pages 5 and 11 are by Peter Bull Design.